Cooperative Learning
structures for
success!

Laurie Kagan &
Dr. Spencer Kagan

Kagan

v1.0 mlk

Kagan Publishing
1160 Calle Cordillera
San Clemente, CA 92673
1 (800) WEE CO-OP • (949) 369-6310
www.KaganOnline.com

Table of Contents

structures for
success!

Laurie & Spencer Kagan: *Cooperative Learning Structures for Success*
Kagan Publishing • 1(800) WEE CO-OP • www.KaganOnline.com

Table of Contents

Overview

In This Section

Welcome,

The following are some tips which can make the workshop more worthwhile.

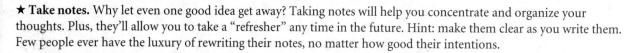

★ **Meet other people.** This is an excellent opportunity to expand your network of contacts. During breaks sit next to someone you don't know, even if you've come with a group. Mingle during the breaks. Exchange ideas. Every participant has a specific area of expertise; find out what it is instead of chatting about the weather. Remember your goal sheet. Why not make it a personal goal to meet at least one person you intend to meet with or talk with on a regular basis following the workshop?

★ **Participate!** Make contributions. Actively participate in the exercises. Consider the meeting room to be a "Mental gymnasium" where it's okay to run, fall and get up again. You'll benefit much more by participating in the game than sitting on the sidelines.

★ **Take notes.** Why let even one good idea get away? Taking notes will help you concentrate and organize your thoughts. Plus, they'll allow you to take a "refresher" any time in the future. Hint: make them clear as you write them. Few people ever have the luxury of rewriting their notes, no matter how good their intentions.

★ **Relate what you learn to your self.** Don't settle for "abstract" knowledge. Have your current problems, conflicts and interests foremost in your mind. As you learn new approaches and techniques, relate them to your own situation.

★ **Find "the big idea."** Occasionally push back from the details and sum it all up. Try to identify at least one "big idea" that alone will make this workshop worthwhile.

★ **Make a commitment to review your notes.** During the workshop set some time aside in the evenings to review your notes. Take out your calendar and make a one hour appointment with yourself for a month from now to "retake" the workshop. Don't put your good ideas away with your notes.

★ **Share your ideas with fellow teachers and your principal.** Share your "major learnings" with someone who can support you. We all need a support person. Enter this as a goal on your "Action Plan."

★ **Enjoy yourself. Relax.** Forget about what's happening at your home or school. This is your workshop. Allow yourself to be here fully. Be yourself. Enjoy.

Sincerely,

Spencer Kagan *Laurie Kagan*

Spencer Kagan and Laurie Kagan
Directors, Kagan Publishing & Professional Development

Laurie & Spencer Kagan: *Cooperative Learning Structures for Success*
Kagan Publishing • 1(800) WEE CO-OP • www.KaganOnline.com

2   Overview

Kagan's "New" Cooperative Learning

Imagine transforming a classroom so that it hums with activity — a classroom in which students work together solving problems, creating projects, constructing knowledge, and demonstrating to each other their new learnings.

Sounds wonderful, doesn't it? But we all know simply putting students in teams does not work. We also know that complex cooperative learning lessons are difficult to implement and are not implemented on a regular basis.

Now, after two decades of research on teaching and learning through cooperative learning, Kagan offers a new approach to staff development workshops and institutes. Kagan's new cooperative learning is transforming teaching and learning. Kagan provides powerful methods which are easy to learn and implement.

Kagan's new approach to cooperative learning avoids the twin traps of group work and cooperative learning lessons. Giving groups a problem to solve, giving teams a group grade, and telling students to discuss a question with a partner are all forms of group work. Group work does not consistently produce positive results and often backfires. Complex cooperative learning lessons do consistently produce positive results, but are seldom implemented. Teachers simply do not have the time to spend every night planning a new cooperative learning lesson.

Kagan charts a NEW course which abandons complex cooperative learning lessons and avoids ineffective group work. This new approach is based on proven, simple cooperative learning structures which become part of every lesson. The structures are easy for teachers to learn and implement, fun for students, and produce dramatic results immediately.

With Kagan, teachers no longer plan cooperative learning lessons; they adopt proven structures which make cooperative learning part of every lesson. Kagan is an integrated approach.

Kagan structures are being used successfully by hundreds of thousands of teachers at every grade level, in all academic areas, and with every type of student. In the Kagan approach, teachers use powerful cooperative learning structures every day, in every lesson — on the average every ten minutes!

Laurie & Spencer Kagan: *Cooperative Learning Structures for Success*
Kagan Publishing • 1(800) WEE CO-OP • www.KaganOnline.com

Overview

Why Learn Kagan?

You will...

- *Experience the power of teamwork and support*

- *Have more quality time with students*

- *Have more fun teaching*

- *Side-step discipline traps*

- *Learn efficient management tools*

- *Create the will to work together among students*

- *Hold every student individually accountable in every activity*

- *Create equal participation; eliminate free-riders*

- *Dramatically increase active participation*

- *Motivate and entice at-risk learners*

- *Dramatically accelerate student learning, grades, and test scores*

- *Spend less time on classroom management*

- *Draw from a storehouse of easy to implement strategies*

- *Engage students with all patterns of multiple intelligences*

- *Create dynamic learning experiences*

Kagan structures have been adopted and are being used with success in schools and districts worldwide. Recently, in an intensive worldwide selection process, a large, urban Canadian district, which makes very extensive use of Kagan, was selected as the top school district in the world!

Dr. Kagan's book, *Cooperative Learning,* is the most popular and comprehensive book in the field. It has sold a quarter of a million copies!

Kagan's approach is in contrast to replacement models. Other approaches to staff development ask teachers to stop teaching the way they are currently teaching and to adopt a new way of teaching. This replacement cycle leads to the familiar syndrome in which teachers learn to dismiss each new staff development opportunity as "This Year's New Thing." Kagan's approach is different. It is an integrated approach which is incorporated into existing lessons. Teachers are not asked to toss away carefully developed lessons; they learn to deliver all lessons through powerful new structures. With the Kagan approach teachers are invited to add to their storehouse of skills; they are not told to abandon their present practices in favor of new methods.

Staff development based on the Kagan approach produces dramatic, proven results with relatively little investment. Resistance among teachers evaporates because the methods are easy to learn. Students profit from the highly structured methods in many ways: academically, socially, and in their self-esteem. Ethnic relations improve dramatically. The Kagan structures prepare students for life in the 21st Century which will be marked by diversity and teamwork.

Laurie & Spencer Kagan: *Cooperative Learning Structures for Success*
Kagan Publishing • 1(800) WEE CO-OP • www.KaganOnline.com

structures for SUCCESS!

workshop Agenda

Day 1	Day 2
• Overview	• Revisit-Rebuild
• Classbuilding	• Domain of Usefulness
• Teambuilding	• Review
• Rationale	• RoundTable Family
• Model Teacher ABC	• Brain Breaks
• Cooperative Learning vs. Group Work	• Six Key Concepts
• Testing PIES	• Wrap
• Forming Teams	
• Review	

Laurie & Spencer Kagan: *Cooperative Learning Structures for Success*
Kagan Publishing • 1(800) WEE CO-OP • www.KaganOnline.com

Overview

Three Goals for This Workshop

③ Brain-Compatible

_____ Building
_____ Building
_____ Sports
&_____ Games
_____ Breaks

① Vision

_____

vs.

_____

Not _____ Work
Not _____ Lessons

② Structures

To Generate Activities:

_____
+ _____

• No _____ Prep
• Every _____ Minutes
• Content _____
• Part of _____ Lesson

Laurie & Spencer Kagan: *Cooperative Learning Structures for Success*
Kagan Publishing • 1(800) WEE CO-OP • www.KaganOnline.com

6   Overview

Hot Tips

Laurie & Spencer Kagan: *Cooperative Learning Structures for Success*
Kagan Publishing • 1(800) WEE CO-OP • www.KaganOnline.com

Overview 7

Reflections

Laurie & Spencer Kagan: *Cooperative Learning Structures for Success*
Kagan Publishing • 1(800) WEE CO-OP • www.KaganOnline.com

8   Overview

Free
Page

Free
Page

Laurie & Spencer Kagan: *Cooperative Learning Structures for Success*
Kagan Publishing • 1(800) WEE CO-OP • www.KaganOnline.com

10   Overview

Theory

In This Section

Laurie & Spencer Kagan: *Cooperative Learning Structures for Success*

Kagan Publishing • 1(800) WEE CO-OP • www.KaganOnline.com

Teacher A Traditional	Teacher B Group Work	Teacher C Cooperative Learning
P Positive Interdependence		
I		
E		
S		

Teacher A

Laurie & Spencer Kagan: *Cooperative Learning Structures for Success*
Kagan Publishing • 1(800) WEE CO-OP • www.KaganOnline.com

Theory 13

Teacher B

Teacher C

Free Page

4 Basic Principles

P P_____ I_____

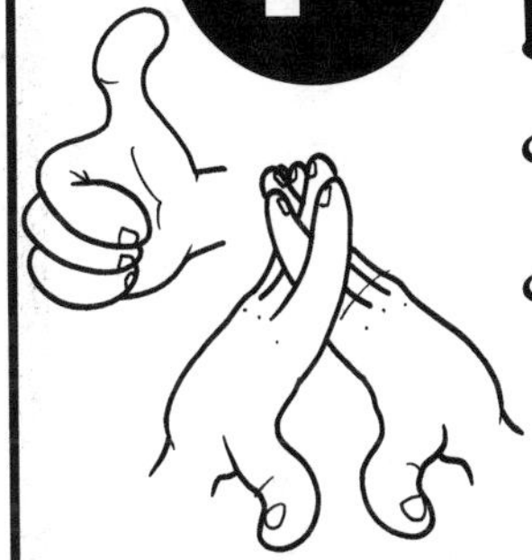

"Is my _____ your _____?"

"Is _____ _____?"

I I_____ A_____

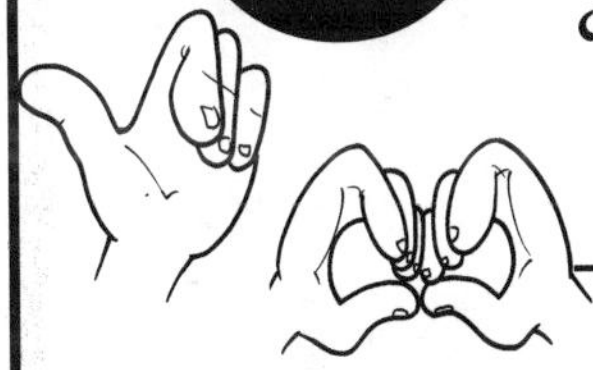

"Is _____ _____ performance

_____?"

E E_____ P_____

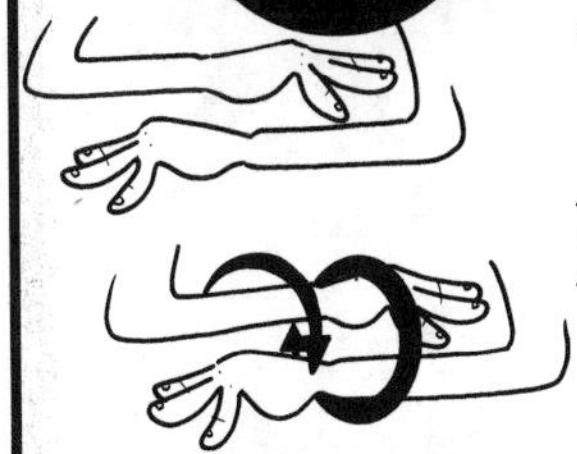

"_____ _____ is the

participation?"

S S_____ I_____

"_____ _____ are

_____active at once?"

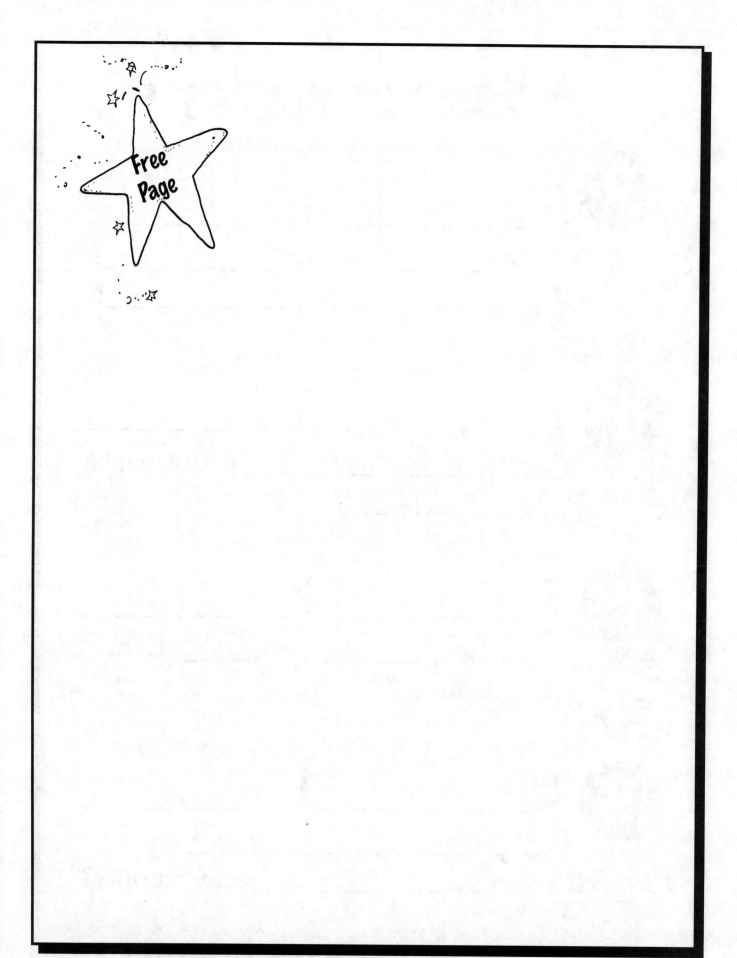

Free Page

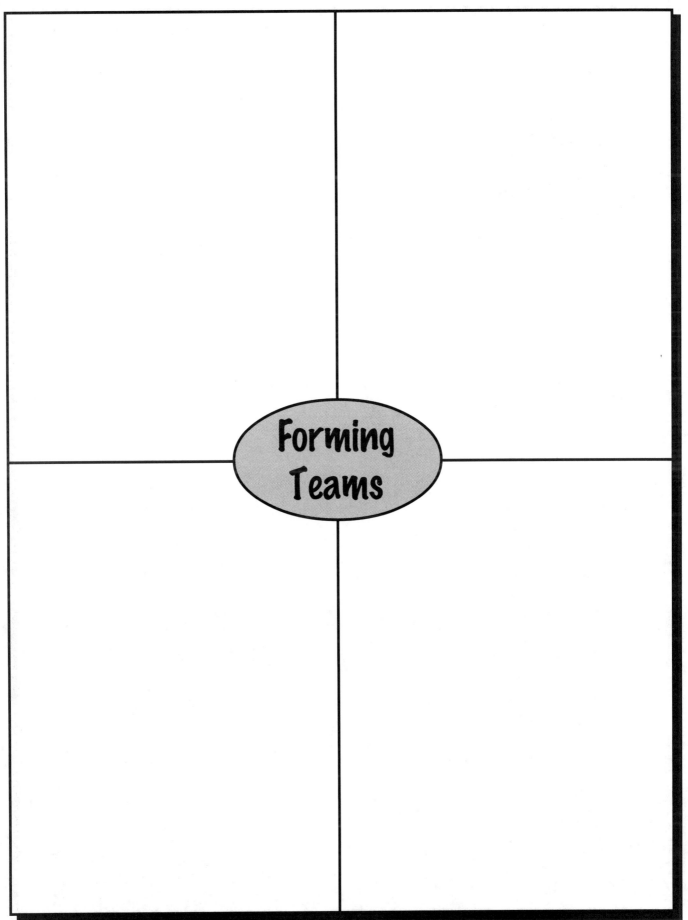

Forming Teams

Free Page

Six Key Concepts

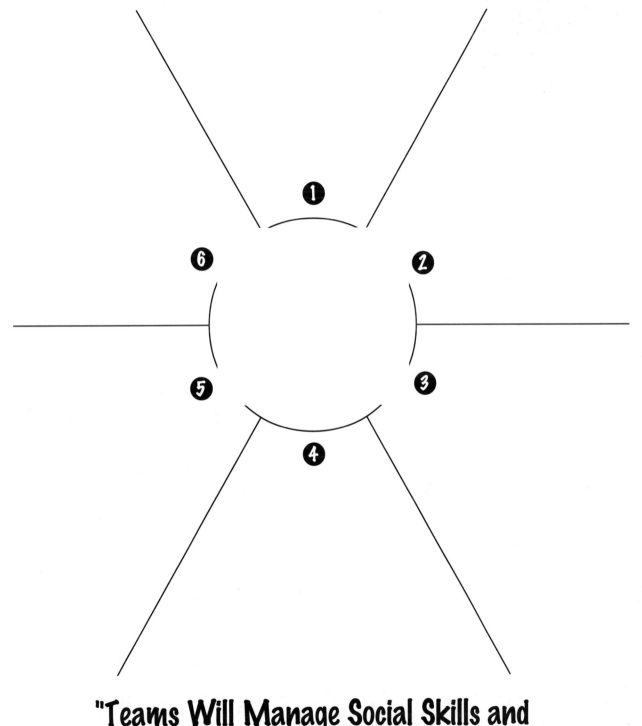

"Teams Will Manage Social Skills and Principles through Structures"

Laurie & Spencer Kagan: *Cooperative Learning Structures for Success*
Kagan Publishing • 1(800) WEE CO-OP • www.KaganOnline.com

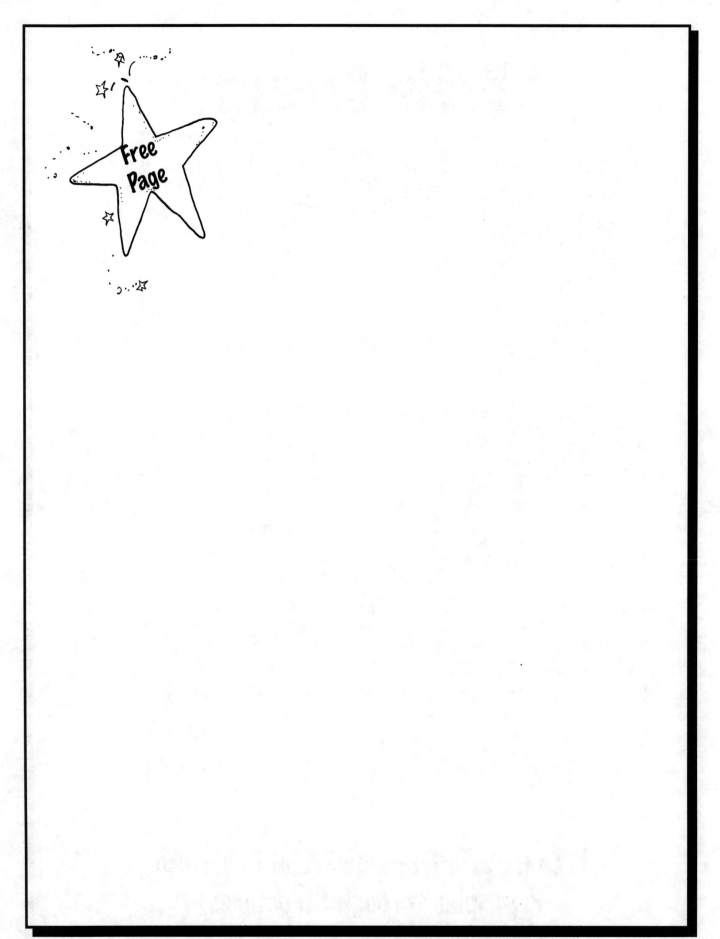

Free
Page

Brain Breaks

Mirror Music

Reasons for Brain Breaks:

-
-
-
-
-
-

Laurie & Spencer Kagan: *Cooperative Learning Structures for Success*
Kagan Publishing • 1(800) WEE CO-OP • www.KaganOnline.com

Theory   23

Brain Breaks

Laurie & Spencer Kagan: *Cooperative Learning Structures for Success*
Kagan Publishing • 1(800) WEE CO-OP • www.KaganOnline.com

24   Overview

Structures

In This Section

Laurie & Spencer Kagan: *Cooperative Learning Structures for Success*
Kagan Publishing • 1(800) WEE CO-OP • www.KaganOnline.com

The Structures   25

What Are the Domains of Usefulness?

Teambuilding

Thinking Skills

Mastery

Classbuilding

Communication Skills

- *Regulators*

- *Builders*

- *Decision Makers*

Information Sharing

I. Among Teammates
II. Among Teams
III. Team to Team

Laurie & Spencer Kagan: *Cooperative Learning Structures for Success*
Kagan Publishing • 1(800) WEE CO-OP • www.KaganOnline.com

26   **The Structures**

Domains Chart

Structures	Classbuilding	Teambuilding	Mastery	Thinking Skills	Communication Skills	Information Sharing	Decision Making	Size
Fan-N-Pick		●	●	●	●			T
Mix-N-Match	●		●					C
Mix Pair Share	●			●		●		C
Numbered Heads Together			●	●			D	T
RallyCoach			●	●	●			P
RallyRobin			●	●	●			P
RallyTable			●	●	●			P
RoundRobin		●	●	●	●	●		T
RoundTable		●	●	●	●	●		T
Simultaneous RoundTable		●	●	●	●	●		T
Stand Up, Hand Up, Pair Up	●		●	●	●	●		P
Talking Chips					●			T
Team Stand-N-Share					●	●		C
Timed Pair Share				●	●	●		P

structures for **SUCCESS!**

Fan-N-Pick

Students play a card game to respond to questions.

STEPS

Set-Up: *Each team receives a set of question cards.*

1 _____ _____ holds question cards in a fan and says "Pick a card, any card!"

2 _____ _____ picks a card, reads the question out loud and allows five seconds of Think Time.

3 Student Three _____ the question.

4 Student Four _____ to the answer:
- For right or wrong answers, Student Four checks and then either praises or _____.
- For higher-level thinking questions which have no right or wrong answer, Student Four does not check for correctness, but _____ and paraphrases the thinking that went into the answer.

5 Students _____ roles one clockwise for each new round.

Laurie & Spencer Kagan: *Cooperative Learning Structures for Success*
Kagan Publishing • 1(800) WEE CO-OP • www.KaganOnline.com

28   **The Structures**

social
SKILLS

IDEAS
...for my class!

management
TIPS

- ☐ Teambuilding
- ☐ Classbuilding
- ☐ Mastery
- ☐ Thinking Skills
- ☐ Communication Skills
- ☐ Information Sharing

Laurie & Spencer Kagan: *Cooperative Learning Structures for Success*
Kagan Publishing • 1(800) WEE CO-OP • www.KaganOnline.com

The Structures 29

Mix-N-Match

Students mix, repeatedly quizzing new partners and trading cards. Afterwards, they rush to find a partner with the card that matches theirs.

STEPS

Set-Up: *Each student needs one card that is a match to another student's card.*

1 With a card in their hand, each student _____ around the room. Each finds a _____, and quizzes him or her by asking a question relating to their card. *(Example: "I have Nevada. What's the capital?" or "I have Sacramento, what's the state?")*

2 Partner _____. Praise or coaching is given.

3 Switch roles: The other _____ asks then praises or coaches.

4 Partners _____ cards.

5 Partners _____ __ and repeat Steps 1 through 4 a number of times.

6 Teacher calls _____!

7 Students freeze, hide their cards, and _____ of their match.

8 Students move to the center of the room, find their match, and quickly move away from the center of the room with their ___ _____.

Optional: Teacher may post a class graph to record the time it takes for students to find their matching partners. Students try to beat their class record.

Laurie & Spencer Kagan: *Cooperative Learning Structures for Success*
Kagan Publishing • 1 (800) WEE CO-OP • www.KaganOnline.com

30   **The Structures**

social SKILLS

IDEAS ...*for my class!*

management TIPS

☐ Teambuilding
☐ Classbuilding
☐ Mastery
☐ Thinking Skills
☐ Communication Skills
☐ Information Sharing

Laurie & Spencer Kagan: *Cooperative Learning Structures for Success*
Kagan Publishing • 1(800) WEE CO-OP • www.KaganOnline.com

Mix Pair Share

Students pair with classmates to discuss the question posed by the teacher.

STEPS

Set-Up: Teacher prepares discussion questions to ask students.

1 Students silently ___ around the room.

2 Teacher calls _____.

3 Students pair up with the person closest to them and shake hands. Students who haven't found a partner ____ their ____ to find each other.

4 Teacher asks a question and gives _____ ____.

5 Students share with their partners using:
- ____ ___ ____
- _____

Laurie & Spencer Kagan: *Cooperative Learning Structures for Success*
Kagan Publishing • 1(800) WEE CO-OP • www.KaganOnline.com

social SKILLS

IDEAS
for my class!

management TIPS

- [ ] Teambuilding
- [ ] Classbuilding
- [ ] Mastery
- [ ] Thinking Skills
- [ ] Communication Skills
- [ ] Information Sharing

Laurie & Spencer Kagan: *Cooperative Learning Structures for Success*
Kagan Publishing • 1(800) WEE CO-OP • www.KaganOnline.com

The Structures 33

Numbered Heads Together

Teammates work together to ensure all members understand; one is randomly selected to be held accountable.

STEPS

Set-Up: *Teacher prepares questions or problems to ask teams.*

1 Students _____ ___.

2 Teacher poses a problem and gives _____ _____.
(*Example: "Everyone think about how rainbows are formed. [Pause] Now make sure everyone in your team knows how rainbows are formed."*)

3 Students lift up from their chairs to put their _____ _____, discuss and teach.

4 Students sit down when _____ knows the answer or has something to share.

5 Teacher calls a _____. The student with that number from each team answers _____, using:
- Slate Share
- Choral Practice
- Finger Responses
- Chalkboard Responses
- Response Cards
- Manipulatives

6 Teammates _____ students who responded.

Laurie & Spencer Kagan: *Cooperative Learning Structures for Success*
Kagan Publishing • 1(800) WEE CO-OP • www.KaganOnline.com

34   The Structures

social SKILLS

IDEAS *for my class!*

management TIPS

- [ ] **Teambuilding**
- [ ] **Classbuilding**
- [ ] **Mastery**
- [ ] **Thinking Skills**
- [ ] **Communication Skills**
- [ ] **Information Sharing**

Laurie & Spencer Kagan: *Cooperative Learning Structures for Success*
Kagan Publishing • 1(800) WEE CO-OP • www.KaganOnline.com

The Structures   35

RallyCoach

Partners take turns, one solving a problem while the other coaches.

STEPS

Set-Up: *1 set of problems, 1 pencil per pair.*

1 The teacher poses a _____ to which there is ____ correct answer.

2 Partner A solves the _____; Partner B watches, _____, and praises.

3 Teacher poses the ____ problem.

4 Partner B _____ the problem; Partner A watches, _____, and praises.

5 Repeat starting at ____ _.

Laurie & Spencer Kagan: *Cooperative Learning Structures for Success*
Kagan Publishing • 1(800) WEE CO-OP • www.KaganOnline.com

36   **The Structures**

social SKILLS

IDEAS
#for my class!

management **TIPS**

- ☐ Teambuilding
- ☐ Classbuilding
- ☐ Mastery
- ☐ Thinking Skills
- ☐ Communication Skills
- ☐ Information Sharing

Laurie & Spencer Kagan: *Cooperative Learning Structures for Success*
Kagan Publishing • 1(800) WEE CO-OP • www.KaganOnline.com

The Structures　37

RallyRobin

In pairs, students alternate generating oral responses.

STEPS

1 Teacher poses a problem to which there are _____ possible responses or _____.

2 In pairs, students _____ _____ stating responses or solutions _____.

Laurie & Spencer Kagan: *Cooperative Learning Structures for Success*
Kagan Publishing • 1(800) WEE CO-OP • www.KaganOnline.com

38   The Structures

social SKILLS

IDEAS
for my class!

management TIPS

- [ ] **Teambuilding**
- [ ] **Classbuilding**
- [ ] **Mastery**
- [ ] **Thinking Skills**
- [ ] **Communication Skills**
- [ ] **Information Sharing**

Laurie & Spencer Kagan: *Cooperative Learning Structures for Success*
Kagan Publishing • 1(800) WEE CO-OP • www.KaganOnline.com

Rally Table

In pairs, students alternate generating written responses or solving problems.

STEPS

Set-Up: 1 paper, 1 pencil per pair.

1 Teacher poses a _____ or provides a task to which there are _____ possible answers, steps, or procedures.

2 In _____, students take turns _____ the paper and pencil or team project, each writing one answer or making a contribution.

Laurie & Spencer Kagan: *Cooperative Learning Structures for Success*
Kagan Publishing • 1(800) WEE CO-OP • www.KaganOnline.com

40 **The Structures**

social SKILLS

IDEAS
for my class!

management TIPS

☐ **Teambuilding**
☐ **Classbuilding**
☐ **Mastery**
☐ **Thinking Skills**
☐ **Communication Skills**
☐ **Information Sharing**

Laurie & Spencer Kagan: *Cooperative Learning Structures for Success*
Kagan Publishing • 1(800) WEE CO-OP • www.KaganOnline.com

The Structures 41

RoundRobin

In teams, students take turns responding orally.

STEPS

1 Teacher assigns a topic or question with _____ possible answers.

2 In teams, students respond _____, each in turn taking about the same amount of time.

Laurie & Spencer Kagan: *Cooperative Learning Structures for Success*
Kagan Publishing • 1(800) WEE CO-OP • www.KaganOnline.com

42   **The Structures**

social SKILLS

IDEAS *for my class!*

management **TIPS**

- [ ] Teambuilding
- [ ] Classbuilding
- [ ] Mastery
- [ ] Thinking Skills
- [ ] Communication Skills
- [ ] Information Sharing

RoundTable

In teams, students take turns generating written responses, solving problems, or making a contribution to the team project.

STEPS

Set-Up: 1 paper, 1 pencil per team.

1 Teacher poses a _____, a question with ____ possible answers, or a topic to write about, or a task to which there are many possible solutions, steps, or procedures.

2 In teams, students ____ _____ passing the paper and pencil or team project, each writing one answer or making a contribution.

Laurie & Spencer Kagan: *Cooperative Learning Structures for Success*
Kagan Publishing • 1(800) WEE CO-OP • www.KaganOnline.com

IDEAS
 # for my class!

social
SKILLS

management
TIPS

☐ **Teambuilding**
☐ **Classbuilding**
☐ **Mastery**
☐ **Thinking Skills**
☐ **Communication Skills**
☐ **Information Sharing**

Laurie & Spencer Kagan: *Cooperative Learning Structures for Success*
Kagan Publishing • 1(800) WEE CO-OP • www.KaganOnline.com

Simultaneous RoundTable

In teams, students simultaneously generate responses then pass their list or product clockwise so each teammate can add to the prior responses.

STEPS

Set-Up: 4 papers, 4 pencils per team of 4.

1 Teacher _____ a topic or question.

2 All four students respond _____ writing or drawing.

3 Teacher signals ____, or students place _____ ___ when done with the problem.

4 Students ____ papers one person _____.

5 Students _____ writing or drawing, _____ to what was already on the paper.

6 Continue, starting at Step 3.

Alternative: Students may _____ their responses with manipulatives rather than draw or write.

Laurie & Spencer Kagan: *Cooperative Learning Structures for Success*
Kagan Publishing • 1(800) WEE CO-OP • www.KaganOnline.com

46   **The Structures**

social SKILLS

IDEAS *for my class!*

management TIPS

- ☐ Teambuilding
- ☐ Classbuilding
- ☐ Mastery
- ☐ Thinking Skills
- ☐ Communication Skills
- ☐ Information Sharing

Laurie & Spencer Kagan: *Cooperative Learning Structures for Success*
Kagan Publishing • 1(800) WEE CO-OP • www.KaganOnline.com

The Structures 47

Stand Up,
Hand Up, Pair Up

Students stand up, put their hands up, and quickly find a partner.

STEPS

1 Teacher says "_____ up, _____ up, and _____ up!"

2 Students stand up and keep one _____ in the air until they find the_____ partner who's not a _____.

3 Teacher gives the _____ or assignment.

4 Teacher provides _____ _____.

5 _____ share using:
• Pair Discussion
• RallyRobin
• Timed Pair Share

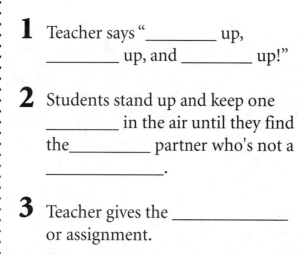

Laurie & Spencer Kagan: *Cooperative Learning Structures for Success*
Kagan Publishing • 1(800) WEE CO-OP • www.KaganOnline.com

48   The Structures

social
SKILLS

IDEAS
for my class!

management
TIPS

☐ Teambuilding
☐ Classbuilding
☐ Mastery
☐ Thinking Skills
☐ Communication Skills
☐ Information Sharing

Laurie & Spencer Kagan: *Cooperative Learning Structures for Success*
Kagan Publishing • 1(800) WEE CO-OP • www.KaganOnline.com

Talking Chips

Students place their chip in the center each time they talk. They cannot talk again until all teammembers have placed a chip.

STEPS

Set-Up: Teams have talking chips (Maximum: two chips each). Talking chips may be pencils, card board chips, tokens, or pogs.

1 Teacher provides a _____ topic.

2 Any student _____ the discussion, placing his or her _____ in the center of the team table.

3 Any student with a _____ continues _____, using his or her chip.

4 When all _____ are used, teammates all _____ their chips and continue the discussion using their talking chips.

Laurie & Spencer Kagan: *Cooperative Learning Structures for Success*
Kagan Publishing • 1(800) WEE CO-OP • www.KaganOnline.com

50   **The Structures**

IDEAS *#for my class!*

social SKILLS

management T I P S

☐ **Teambuilding**
☐ **Classbuilding**
☐ **Mastery**
☐ **Thinking Skills**
☐ **Communication Skills**
☐ **Information Sharing**

Laurie & Spencer Kagan: *Cooperative Learning Structures for Success*
Kagan Publishing • 1(800) WEE CO-OP • www.KaganOnline.com

The Structures 51

Team Stand-N-Share

Teams stand to share their answers with the class.

STEPS

Set-Up: Teams have a list of items to share.

1 All students stand near their _____.

2 Teacher calls on a _____ student. Selected student states one idea from the team list.

3 The student in each team holding their team _____ either _____ the item to the list, or if it is already listed, _____ it off.

4 Students pass their team _____ one teammate clockwise.

5 Teams ___ when all their items are _____. While seated they RoundTable adding each new item as it is _____. When all teams are _____, Team Stand-N-Share is completed.

Laurie & Spencer Kagan: *Cooperative Learning Structures for Success*
Kagan Publishing • 1(800) WEE CO-OP • www.KaganOnline.com

52   **The Structures**

social SKILLS

IDEAS for my class!

management TIPS

- ☐ Teambuilding
- ☐ Classbuilding
- ☐ Mastery
- ☐ Thinking Skills
- ☐ Communication Skills
- ☐ Information Sharing

Laurie & Spencer Kagan: *Cooperative Learning Structures for Success*
Kagan Publishing • 1(800) WEE CO-OP • www.KaganOnline.com

The Structures 53

Timed Pair Share

In pairs, students share with a partner for a predetermined time while the partner listens carefully. Then partners switch roles.

STEPS

1 Teacher announces a topic and states ___ ____ each student will have to share.

2 Teacher provides _____ ____.

3 In pairs, Partner A _____; Partner B _____.

4 Partner B _____. *(Example: "Thanks for sharing." "One thing I learned as I listened to you was…")*

5 Pairs switch roles: Partner B _____; Partner A _____.

6 Partner A _____.

Laurie & Spencer Kagan: *Cooperative Learning Structures for Success*
Kagan Publishing • 1(800) WEE CO-OP • www.KaganOnline.com

54   **The Structures**

social SKILLS

IDEAS *for my class!*

management **TIPS**

- ☐ **Teambuilding**
- ☐ **Classbuilding**
- ☐ **Mastery**
- ☐ **Thinking Skills**
- ☐ **Communication Skills**
- ☐ **Information Sharing**

Laurie & Spencer Kagan: *Cooperative Learning Structures for Success*
Kagan Publishing • 1(800) WEE CO-OP • www.KaganOnline.com

The Structures 55

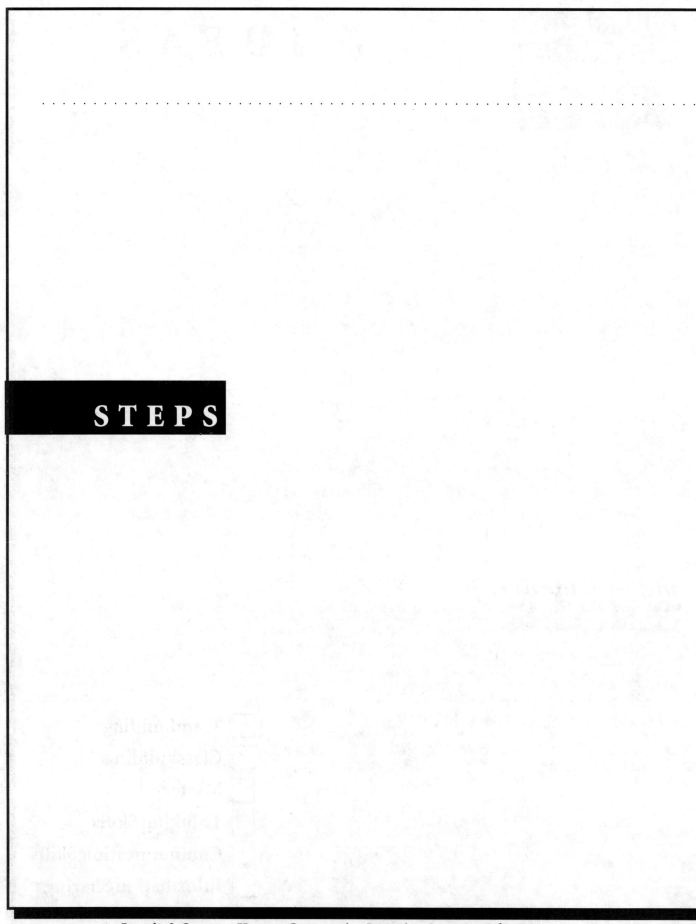

STEPS

Laurie & Spencer Kagan: *Cooperative Learning Structures for Success*
Kagan Publishing • 1(800) WEE CO-OP • www.KaganOnline.com

56   **The Structures**

IDEAS ...for my class!

social **SKILLS**

management **TIPS**

☐ **Teambuilding**
☐ **Classbuilding**
☐ **Mastery**
☐ **Thinking Skills**
☐ **Communication Skills**
☐ **Information Sharing**

Laurie & Spencer Kagan: *Cooperative Learning Structures for Success*
Kagan Publishing • 1(800) WEE CO-OP • www.KaganOnline.com

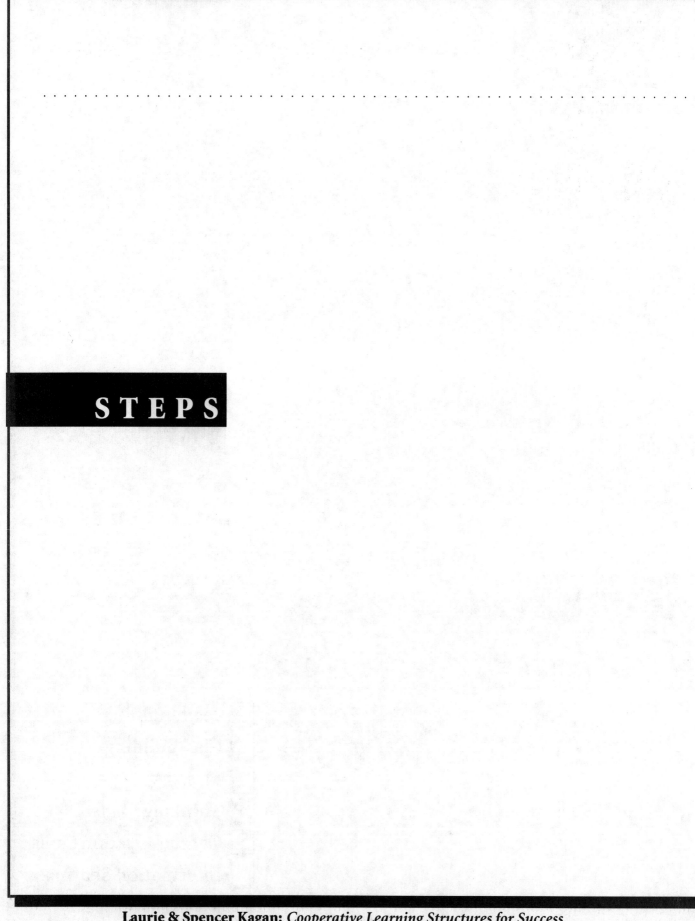

STEPS

social **SKILLS**

IDEAS
#for my class!

management **TIPS**

- ☐ Teambuilding
- ☐ Classbuilding
- ☐ Mastery
- ☐ Thinking Skills
- ☐ Communication Skills
- ☐ Information Sharing

Laurie & Spencer Kagan: *Cooperative Learning Structures for Success*

Kagan Publishing • 1(800) WEE CO-OP • www.KaganOnline.com

STEPS

social SKILLS

IDEAS
#for my class!

management TIPS

- [ ] Teambuilding
- [ ] Classbuilding
- [ ] Mastery
- [ ] Thinking Skills
- [ ] Communication Skills
- [ ] Information Sharing

Laurie & Spencer Kagan: *Cooperative Learning Structures for Success*
Kagan Publishing • 1(800) WEE CO-OP • www.KaganOnline.com

The Structures   61

Free
Page

Laurie & Spencer Kagan: *Cooperative Learning Structures for Success*
Kagan Publishing • 1(800) WEE CO-OP • www.KaganOnline.com

62   **The Structures**

Resources

In This Section

Laurie & Spencer Kagan: *Cooperative Learning Structures for Success*
Kagan Publishing • 1(800) WEE CO-OP • www.KaganOnline.com

Resources   63

Kagan Online Magazine

A FREE Quarterly Magazine on the Internet.

Each quarter, *Kagan Publishing & Professional Development* posts a new Kagan Online Magazine on the Kagan Website. You will find helpful teacher and trainer tips, step-by-step structures, downloadable activities, provocative articles, action research by Kagan practitioners, reviews of the latest Kagan products, professional development opportunities in your area, humorous education anecdotes and jokes, and hot links to other great teacher stuff on the Web. And did we mention it's FREE?

FEATURES

- **Teacher Tips**
- **Trainer Tips**
- **Structures**
- **Activities**
- **Articles**
- **Research**
- **New Products**
- **Workshops**
- **Anecdotes**
- **Hot Links**

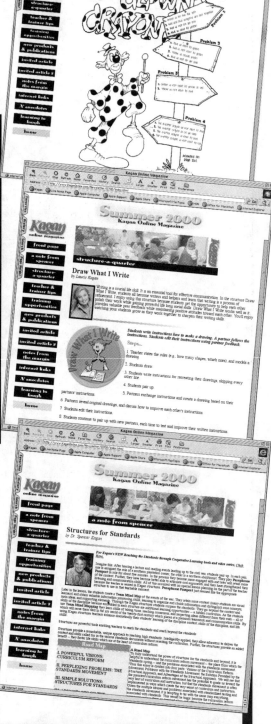

Visit www.KaganOnline.com for your FREE Subscription!

Host A Kagan Event

Kagan proudly offers a variety of professional development opportunities your school or district may host. Choose the best format for your teachers from a wide selection of exciting topics. Your teachers will receive world-class training at a site of your choice. Hosts must meet a minimum number of participants for the training, and provide the training location or help us find one. Hosts and facilitators earn money and/or vouchers toward the purchase of training materials.

Kagan Professional Development Events

Available as 1-day, 2-day, or week-long institutes.

▷ **Cooperative Learning**

▷ **Multiple Intelligences**

▷ **Win-Win Discipline**

▷ **Character Development & Emotional Intelligence**

▷ **Secondary Block**

▷ **New Teachers**

▷ **Training for Trainers**

How to Host A Kagan Event

1 Select the **Kagan Professional Development Event** of your choice

2 Call **Nancy Murray, Director of Kagan Professional Development**
1 (800) 451-8495

3 Enjoy your school or district's best-ever professional development event

---

Laurie & Spencer Kagan: *Cooperative Learning Structures for Success*
Kagan Publishing • 1(800) WEE CO-OP • www.KaganOnline.com

Professional Development Opportunities

Kagan

Cooperative Learning

Learn Kagan's easy cooperative structures. The focus of this in-service is instructional strategies to use as part of any lesson with little or no teacher preparation. You'll learn the basics of teamformation, teambuilding, classbuilding, management, scoring and recognition, assessment, the PIES principles, and a range of dynamic cooperative learning structures.

Multiple Intelligences

Teach to all eight intelligences, develop all intelligences, and create in every student an understanding and appreciation of their own unique pattern of intelligences as well as that of others. Learn simple structures which release the power of MI in any lesson.

Win-Win Discipline

Learn a host of strategies to use in the moment of a classroom disruption and what to do afterwards to prevent future classroom disruptions. Build student self-esteem, teach responsibility, and enhance engagement.

Emotional Intelligence

Boost your students' emotional intelligence. Deepen students' understanding of their own emotions. Learn and apply the Kagan Taxonomy of Emotions. Help students control their emotions and act rationally rather than impulsively. Encourage students to motivate themselves. Promote empathy. Develop students' social skills and character.

Character Development

Learn to promote the range of positive character traits through proven cooperative learning and social skill methods. Foster responsible and respectful behaviors as part of every lesson, with little or no special preparation.

To host any of these events, bring Dr. Spencer Kagan, Laurie Kagan or a Nationally Certified Kagan trainer to your school, call Nancy Murray, Director of Kagan Professional Development 1 (800) 451-8495

Block Scheduling and Secondary Restructuring

Leave this training ready to implement proven structures for today's secondary school students. Learn structures which create a total engagement for the entire block.

Hands-On Science

Teach science content and science process skills through easy-to-learn, easy-to-use hands-on cooperative learning structures.

Teambuilding and Classbuilding

Build caring and cooperative teams with teambuilding structures and activities. Your classroom becomes a caring community in which each student feels known, accepted, and appreciated.

Math with Manipulatives

Implement the best of NCTM standards, teaching every math concept at the concrete, connecting, and symbolic level. Teach for understanding through a range of powerful cooperative learning math structures.

Laurie & Spencer Kagan: *Cooperative Learning Structures for Success*
Kagan Publishing • 1(800) WEE CO-OP • www.KaganOnline.com

Kagan Professional Development Opportunities

Creating the Cooperative School

Administrators and lead teachers learn proven methods to bring staff, students, and administrators together to create the cooperative school.

Higher-Level Thinking Strategies and Manipulatives

Stimulate higher-level thinking through simple cooperative question prompts used across the range of curriculum areas. Learn to use the Question Spinners and Matrix, Spin-N-Think, Story Switchers, Higher-Level Thinking Question Cards, and the Idea Spinner. Your classroom becomes a think tank with cooperative learning structures and manipulatives.

The Multicultural Classroom

Kagan instructional structures are the natural way to create a caring classroom that honors and celebrates diversity. Learn research-based methods which improve race relations and create a cooperative classroom community.

Peer Coaching for Teachers

The best predictor of sustained implementation of educational innovations is peer coaching. Peer coaching enables change while holding teachers accountable for implementation. Learn models of peer coaching which provide the necessary pressure and support for change.

Cooperative Learning in the Primary Classroom

Primary teachers love our "lessons for little ones." Learn how to promote social and academic gains through proven structures for primary students.

Second Language Learning through Cooperative Learning

Your second-language learners acquire English or any other second language with ease through dozens of cooperative and communicative structures. Designed for ESL and foreign language teachers.

Social Studies

Teach to the themes recommended by the National Council of Social Studies through proven cooperative learning and multiple intelligences methods. Students learn the fundamental principles of democracy, through cooperative, democratic classroom structures.

Creating the Inclusive Classroom

Kagan's cooperative structures create an inclusive, cooperative community for all students. Learn special adaptations for the range of special need students.

Kagan structures for **success!**

Laurie & Spencer Kagan: *Cooperative Learning Structures for Success*

Kagan Publishing • 1(800) WEE CO-OP • www.KaganOnline.com

Featured Products

Cooperative Learning

Dr. Spencer Kagan (All Grades)

Practical and easy-to-use, this classic (over one quarter of a million copies in print) has been acclaimed as the single most comprehensive book on cooperative learning. This is the book which is leading teachers world wide to transform their lessons—to make cooperative learning part of every lesson! Have you heard about Numbered Heads Together, Pairs Compare, or Co-op Co-op? Learn about them from the man who created most co-op "structures." Would you like dozens of down-to-earth management tips? How about improving your students' social skills? Or 100's of ready-to-use teambuilding and classbuilding activities to make your class click? This book has it all. You will find easy, step-by-step approaches to teamformation, classroom set-up and management, thinking skills and mastery, lesson planning, scoring and recognition, and research and theory. Tables, graphics and reproducibles make cooperative learning easy, fun, and successful. 392 pages. **BCL • $35**

Cooperative Learning SmartCard

Here's Dr. Spencer Kagan's NEW cooperative learning in a nutshell. This 11" x 17" laminated, colorful reference card includes: the 6 essential keys to make cooperative learning successful in your class; 4 basic principles to implement true cooperative learning; a thumbnail sketch of 56 powerful cooperative strategies; and listings of cooperative strategies to create effective lessons and engage the multiple intelligences. This handy little reference card is highly recommended for anyone purchasing the book Cooperative Learning. **TCL • $3**

To order:

1 (800) WEE CO-OP   Kagan   www.KaganOnline.com

Laurie & Spencer Kagan: *Cooperative Learning Structures for Success*
Kagan Publishing • 1(800) WEE CO-OP • www.KaganOnline.com

68   Resources

Teambuilding

Laurie, Miguel & Spencer Kagan (All Grades)

When students have the desire and ability to work together as a team, something magical happens—**T**ogether **E**veryone **A**chieves **M**ore! Students like working together, academic achievement goes up, and discipline problems become a thing of the past. Includes step-by-step instructions, hints, variations, over 100 teambuilding activities and ready-to-use blackline masters for each of 14 favorite teambuilding structures like: Find-the-Fib, Team Interview, Same-Different. Promote a positive class and team atmosphere in your classroom and watch as your students work together in harmony. 178 pages. **BKT • $25**

Classbuilding

Miguel Kagan, Laurie Robertson
& Spencer Kagan (All Grades)

Create a caring, cooperative class through energizing classbuilding activities! This best-seller includes step-by-step instructions, hints, variations, 100's of activities, and ready-to-use blackline masters for each of 11 favorite cooperative classbuilding structures like: Mix-N-Match, Stir-the-Class, Who-Am-I. A must for the block schedule. Students are quickly and immediately energized—ready to tackle any curriculum. If you want to promote a positive class atmosphere with fun and easy activities, this is the source! 168 pages. **BKC • $25**

SmartCards
$3 each

Laurie & Spencer Kagan: *Cooperative Learning Structures for Success*
Kagan Publishing • 1(800) WEE CO-OP • www.KaganOnline.com

Resources 69

Featured Products

TeachTimer

Just put the TeachTimer on the overhead projector and let it keep track of time for you! The TeachTimer counts either down or up, and sounds and flashes a "Time's Up" alarm. Great for giving students five minutes to write in their journals, two minutes for pairs to discuss a topic, or even 10-15 seconds of think time. Use the built-in chronograph to see how quickly students can line up, make a formation, quiet down, or solve a challenging problem. When it's not in use, the TeachTimer doubles as an overhead clock. A great management tool viewed anywhere in the class. Includes hard protective case and attachment to wear on neck for outdoor use. **WSTIME • $45**

Cooperative Team Slates

(All Grades)

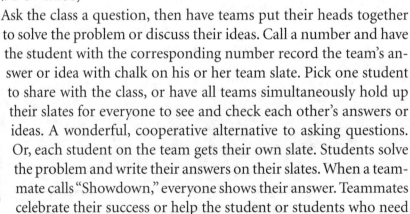

Ask the class a question, then have teams put their heads together to solve the problem or discuss their ideas. Call a number and have the student with the corresponding number record the team's answer or idea with chalk on his or her team slate. Pick one student to share with the class, or have all teams simultaneously hold up their slates for everyone to see and check each other's answers or ideas. A wonderful, cooperative alternative to asking questions. Or, each student on the team gets their own slate. Students solve the problem and write their answers on their slates. When a teammate calls "Showdown," everyone shows their answer. Teammates celebrate their success or help the student or students who need help. Team slates help make learning fun while keeping everyone in the class actively involved! Includes ten 8.5" x 11" black matte boards and ten mini erasers. **WSSE • $10**

Laurie & Spencer Kagan: *Cooperative Learning Structures for Success*
Kagan Publishing • 1(800) WEE CO-OP • www.KaganOnline.com

70   Resources

Selector Overhead Spinners

Select a student. Select a team. Or select any student on any team. Designed for the overhead projector, this transparent spinner is a great way to keep your students actively involved. It includes both the student selector and team selector overhead spinners together on the same convenient spinner! **MSST • $4**

Student Selector Overhead Spinner

Place the Student Selector on the overhead projector and give it a spin. It automatically selects one student from each team even if you have different sized teams working at once! Select one student from each pair, triad, or team of four or five to respond to your question, start the team project, or fill a role such as Materials Monitor. The randomness of the spin ensures that everyone is participating about equally, and it keeps everyone on their toes because students never know who is going to be called on next. This little management tool has been a longtime bestseller! **MSSS • $2**

Team Selector Overhead Spinner

How do you decide which team to call on? Give the Team Selector a spin! It works if your classroom has six, seven, eight or nine teams. The Team Selector is perfect for selecting one team to share their answer or ideas with the class, for choosing which team gives their presentation first, or randomly assigning teams to different projects. Use the Team Selector in tandem with the Student Selector to randomly select one student from the whole class! Another favorite spinner to keep everyone involved. **MSTS • $2**

To order:
1 (800) WEE CO-OP **Kagan** **www.KaganOnline.com**

Laurie & Spencer Kagan: *Cooperative Learning Structures for Success*
Kagan Publishing • 1(800) WEE CO-OP • www.KaganOnline.com

Resources 71

Featured Products

Kagan Cooperative Learning Structures for Success SmartCard

Included in this SmartCard are 28 of Kagan's very best cooperative learning structures. With these structures, you won't have to worry if you're cooperative learning lessons respect the principles known to increase student achievement and improve social relations. These simple, yet powerful structures always work because the basic principles are built in! The structures are easy to learn, easy to use, fun and engaging. Students love them. Achievement increases. Let them work for you. **TSC • $4**

The Teamformation Pocket Chart

One color-coded by achievement.

Team 1	Team 2
Tigers	Lions
Jenny	Laurie
Kent	Juan
Maria	Kelly
Mikey	Bryan

One to post in the class.

Team 1	Team 2
Tigers	Lions
Maria	Bryan
Kent	Juan
Jenny	Kelly
Mikey	Laurie

Creating balanced, heterogeneous cooperative teams is fun and easy. Reassigning students to new heterogeneous teams is also simple with these remarkable manipulatives. The kit includes two sets of T-Cards: one color-coded by achievement, and the other designed to post in your classroom. **MKTFK • $10**

To order:
1 (800) WEE CO-OP **Kagan** **www.KaganOnline.com**

Laurie & Spencer Kagan: *Cooperative Learning Structures for Success*
Kagan Publishing • 1(800) WEE CO-OP • www.KaganOnline.com

Higher-Level Thinking Questions Books Combo Kit

Light the fires of your students' minds with this series of question books. In each book you will find questions, questions, and more questions for sixteen of the most popular themes and topics for that subject. But these are no ordinary questions. They are the important kind—higher-level thinking questions—the kind that stretch your students' minds; the kind that tap your students' natural curiosity about the world; the kind that rack your students' brains; the kind that sharpen your students' thinking skills. Inside you will find a seemingly endless array of intriguing, mind-stretching questions and activities. Each book is spilling over with questions designed to engage and develop the spectrum of higher-level thinking skills. Add an invaluable higher-level thinking component to what you already teach. Make learning exciting, more engaging, and more effective. You can almost see your students' brains growing as they discuss these questions, share their thinking journal entries, and ask and answer their own higher-level thinking questions. Use these books to easily integrate critical and creative thinking skills into your daily lessons. Give your students the most valuable skills they can acquire—the desire to think, and the power to question. 160 pages each. Combo includes all 8 books. *Regular price $152.* Combo price **$109 • CQBC Save $43!** Also available individually:

- Primary Literature, **BQPL • $19**
- Intermediate Literature, **BQIL • $19**
- Language Arts, **BQLA • $19**
- Developing Character, **BQCD • $19**
- Personal & Social Skills, **BQP • $19**
- Physical Science, **BQPS • $19**
- Social Studies, **BQSS • $19**
- Life and Earth Sciences, **BQLS • $19**

Question Cards

Journal Writing

Question Starters

Buy Any 3 Question Books & Get 1 FREE!

To order:

1 (800) WEE CO-OP  **www.KaganOnline.com**

Laurie & Spencer Kagan: *Cooperative Learning Structures for Success*
Kagan Publishing • 1(800) WEE CO-OP • www.KaganOnline.com

Resources 73

Free Page